Druidical Quest
by Dale Bertrand

With excerpts from the manuscripts
of John Hugh Roberts
'The Last Recorder of the Druids'
written in the 19th century

nennius

Azatlan Publishing
Roberts Heritage Foundation
http://www.azatlan.com
© Dale Bertrand 2008

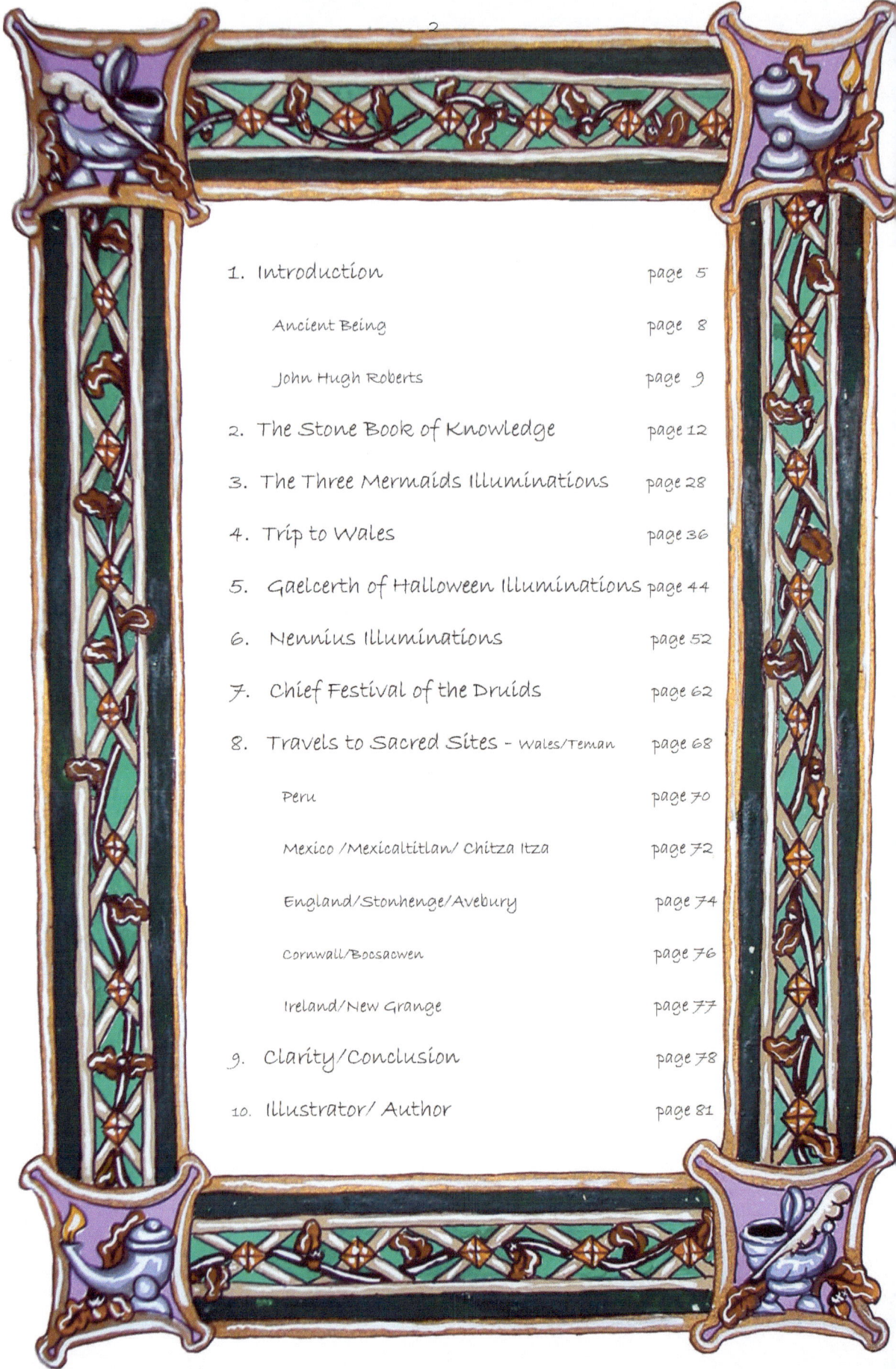

The Land of Mystery and Magic
Gwlad Hyd y Llledrig

There is no place we'd rather visit than
The gleaming streets of crystalled Azatlan
The land that's lost within the mists of Time
That sacred holder of the secret rhyme
That ells the tone that swings inside the stone
To show the Ancient Nennius's gleaming bone
Sat in the chair carved of the living earth
Before the Lirpa Lauph, in which no dearth
Of arcane secrets swell and grow
There in the caverns of the mansion far below
The green and verdant crust of Wales

Bill Meilan October 13, 1981

Druidical Quest

Credits

Author, Book Design and Production   Dale Bertrand
Original Manuscripts written   John H Roberts
Illuminations/Borders   Leo Del Pasqua
Fellow Adventurer & Co-designer   Della Burford
Photography   Della & Dale

Azatlan Publishing
ISBN 978-0-9695611-7-0
Roberts Heritage Foundation
http://www.azatlan.com
Contact: Dale at azatlan@yahoo.com
Distribution: signed copies at www.azatlan.com,
regular copies at www.amazon.com et. al.

Thanks to so many people for helping with this project over the years.
To John Hugh Roberts for his inspirational work.
Dr. David Davies for his integrity and motivation.
Della for her motivation, perseverance and especially for her love.
Everil Helweg Larson-Young & Dr. Henryk Binder for their
wisdom and sense of adventure.
Doug Atkins for his eagle eyes in finding the Stone Book of Knowledge
Mary Bertrand for her love and instilling the love of "history".
Jim Young for saving so many important books from destruction.
Leo Del Pasqua for his wonderful illuminations.
Bill & Patricia Meilan for sharing these mysteries and
for his poetry and love of Wales.
Stevanne for her continued support.
Cayo Evans for his love of Wales and his great Welsh and Irish Whiskies.
Shanti (John) Baldwin for his transcriptions and friendship.
Dr. Jordan Paper for co-journeying to magical North Wales, etc.
Elwyn Roberts and Marian for sharing their home, and the adventure.
Sue Bladon and Barbera Tremain for Cornwall adventures.
To all the Directors of the Roberts Heritage Foundation
Mary Lynn Ogilvie, Edna Reti, Joanne Williams
also Jules Atkins, Tom Williams and all the Williams family
Michael, Pat, Diane, David, Loosie, Howard, Alice, Virgil, Bruce & Ted
To Glen, Brenda and Rob, Laura and kids,
Harri for helping the vision
To all family and friends thank you so much.
I know I have forgotten many others that have contributed
Please forgive me – Thanks to you all
Many of the foregoing people have passed on these last twenty-nine
years ago but each is remembered for their sense of wonder and their
wonderful full lives.

Introduction

Let me tell you a story. It's a true story! Everything I tell you here actually happened! What follows is a journey, a quest to discover more about oneself through intuition and in doing so I discovered unpublished 19th century writings about Druidism by a Welse mystic. But more on that later, now back to the start of the story. In January & February of 1979 Della, my wife, and I were at the Rainbow Rose Festival, ICC Convention at the Pasadena, California Convention Center. We were giving children's workshops around our first book.

Three years earlier I had lost the hearing in my left ear and having been to a variety of doctors, without getting any satisfactory reason as to the cause and permanency of the damage, I arranged to see someone who had been recommended to me as a healer - Dr. David Davies from Abergavenny, Wales. Through a series of unusual events our scheduled meeting was put off 3 times. On the third occasion I returned to the center where workshops were in progress to await the meeting. I happened upon a workshop given by one Rose Gladden from Liverpool, England - also a healer. I entered at 8:40 p.m. and sat down about 15 feet from her in a room of 25-30 people. She was attending to one of the participants but as I did not know what had transpired previously I sat there not altogether interested. At 9:25 she looked at her watch and at that moment her head fell slightly forward and she went into a trance where upon a strange voice came from her, one totally without accent.

An image in her time and space appeared and I, having been a policeman years earlier and a bit of a skeptic of "New Age" things had a difficult few minutes while my intellectual facilities were being jarred by this vision that appeared in her space. The image was of an (first thing that came to mind) Egyptian Oriental face – elongated with a pointed skull and slightly angled eyes. Emanating around it was a gold silver light. I could still see Ms. Gladden there but this being was there in her time and space. During the next two or three minutes I scanned the room for holographic equipment. I looked at faces in the audience. I looked for "a reason" of any kind as I had never had a manifestation happen to me before. What I remember of the words from this being was "It was an ancient that came down through time to appear to certain individuals to guide them into paths of healing." I know more words were spoken but the shock was so great I did not consciously absorb them. Ms. Gladden then snapped out of the trance and was there again in her heavily accented Liverpoolian presence.

I spoke to another person at this workshop on whether she had seen anything or anyone. She had not but had heard a very unusual voice. I was still too shaken to coherently ask what this lady had heard etc.

From here I went and waited for Dr. Davies to come out of a meeting he had been called into at the last moment. At approximately 9:50 p.m. a small 4"9", 90 pound man in a 3 piece wool worsted suit approached me and introduced himself as David Davies. We then went into a room and we spoke for 1 hour about our backgounds and my particular hearing problem. Later in the evening I was recalling the events and suddenly I had an overwhelming feeling that I had to study the Druids. It was so strong that upon my arrival home, I awoke my wife at 2:00 a.m. telling her I had to study the druids.

Four days later I'm on a bus to Vancouver B.C to see my mother. I couldn't tell her of the manifestation and of my strong desire to study the druids as she, being a strong catholic woman, would not understand this sudden desire to study Druidism. During our conversation she mentioned that she had some things that she thought I would be very interested in and she reached under the couch and pulled out an array of old yellowed parchment paper, oil paintings on canvases, watercolors all tumbled together in no order. Right on top in very fine hand writing was a paper titled 'Chief Festival of the Druids' and the next paper was titled 'The Gaelcerth or Bonfire of Halloween'. (My birthday is on Halloween) As I shook with excitement she explained, she had known a man called Charles Steele, (one of the first boys recorded to have been born in Vancouver, B.C.) who passed away at 90 years of age three months earlier. She often went out hunting for antiques with him. When he passed away the executors felt she would appreciate these old manuscripts written by Steeles grandfather and bequeathed them to her. And she then passed them onto me!

Drawing of the Manifestation of the Ancient Being

I sketched this picture of the Ancient Being that I saw in the room in Pasedena California just days after the event. The Being had a slightly pointed head, Oriental eyes and had a radiant aura that shone a silver gold light.

This entity appeared to me in the same time and space as Rose Gladden, a lady from Liverpool England who was giving a workshop on healing energies. I was sitting approximately fifteen feet from this lady when she suddenly went into a trance and this being appeared in her space.

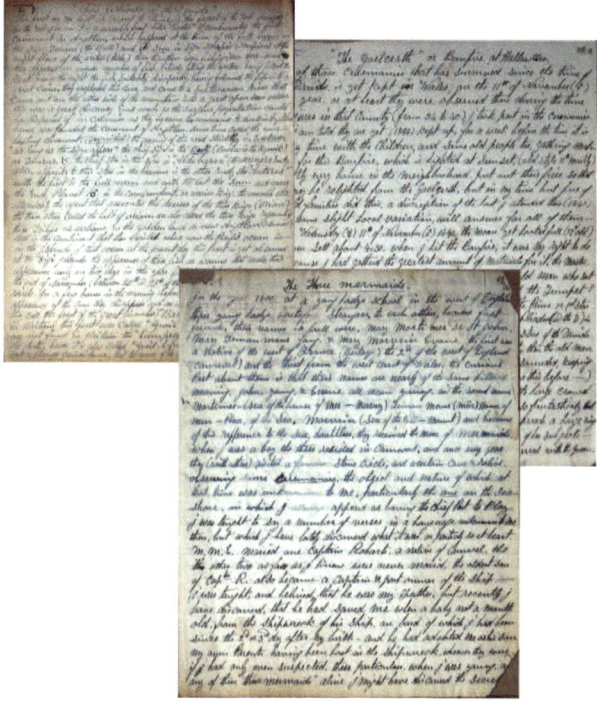

These are the first three manuscripts
I saw–"Chief Festival of the Druids", 'The
Galcerth of Halloween' and 'The Three Mermaids'.
These three manuscripts of four pages each, along with
another titled Nennius, were illuminated and made
into artistic creations by Leo Del Pasqua during
the early 80's. The spelling was not changed from
the originals as there is influence from Robert's
Welsh language and we wanted to keep the
integrity of the originals. Examples follow.

Following exerpted from the Celtic Connection Newspaper

John Hugh Roberts: Mystical Writings from a Cymric Soul

by Dale Bertrand and Della Burford

Early Vancouver was home to many interesting characters: one of these was a Welsh mystique and his family. John Hugh Roberts immigrated to Canada from Wales with his wife Anne in the early 1850s and after exploring various locations in the eastern part of America, settled in Toronto. He was successful at developing property in and around Queen and Sherbourne Street and in 1881 he and his wife Anne Roberts picked up their family, Tomhu, Mississippi, and Sarah, and traveled across Canada to Vancouver, via San Francisco. The family homesteaded on property at what is now Quebec and Tenth Avenue eventually building their dream castle "PenLangera Lodge" in Point Grey and living there until his death in 1917. John Hugh's legacy: Over 55 years of diaries of early Welsh travels and Canadian life in Toronto, in Iowa and in great detail Vancouvers First years from 1884-1917 and also the mysterious papers titled "The Last Recorder of the Druids" and the 'Stone Book of Knowlege'. John Hugh Roberts believed that he was born to Welsh parents in Cornwall in 1828 to a Captain Roberts and his wife. It was not until near his "mothers" death in the 1870s that he learned that he was a foundling,

John Hugh Roberts

saved as an infant off of a shipwreck near Cornwall in 1828. He had been on board from the second or third day of birth and the journey itself had been approx. four weeks. His birth parents drowned and Captain Roberts and family saved him from the raging sea to raise him as their own. He never did discover his birth parents. He was educated and partially raised by three women,

one from Brittany - Mary Mortimer de St. John,

one from Cornwell - Mary Temanmaur Young

and Mary Morvin Evans, from Lllaniestyn North Wales who he undewrstood to be his maternal grandmother.

The three women all had similiar names with the sea or water in them and were referred to as the 'Three Mermaids'. As a foundling, they took him under their wings and he was taught ancient writings and languages, Runes, Oghama, Egyptian Hieroglyphics, Cuneiform writing, Phoenician, Cymric, Gaelic, Greek, modern & ancient Hebrew and other arcane languages.

He writes, that he is one of the, quote "Hereditary Druids (Lords of Teman). We inherit a certain right or privilege under the covenant, provided we conform to certain ordinances. Among these rights are the privileges of reading these wonderful records of nearly 73 hundred years!" unquote.

In the year 1838 he was led to a cave in Cornwell by the two remaining 'Mermaids' and here he was shown many stone slates. He wrote, " there were many written in these Greek letters, and others in Cuneiform hieroglyphics, and others with pictures, and emblems and scrolls. So that I became familiar with them by sight, but was ignorant of their content."

Later in his life he received a charm of which he writes, "enclosed in the charm, a key to these hieroglyphics! And for the last nine years, I devoted all my time to the study and translation, of these ancient Secret Inspiration, and Revelations." These nine years of John Hugh Roberts life were spent in Vancouver. He died in 1917.

This article was written for the Celtic Connection newspaper.

The Stone Book of Knowledge

I was living in Toronto and wondering what to do with these writings and if and how they should be shared with the world. We spent 7 years trying to understand them but over 70% of the papers were missing and the gaps were just too large. Our friends Tom and Sal Williams returned from a vacation on Salt spring Island B.C. and handed me a book, and to my great surprise and shock I immediately realized it was writted by John Hugh Roberts. This book 254 hand written pages was the key to understanding his writings. Doug Atkins, our great friend, found it at the recycling depot at the dump at Ganges, Saltspring Island weeks before and immediately recognized the handwriting as Roberts. This was seven years later after my receiving the manuscripts from my mother. Roberts called it the" Stone Book of Knowledge" and he clearly says that when the time is right – 60 years after 1893 when a covenant ended these records where to be made public. This was another example of the very strange synchronistic events that have occured over the last 29 years.

Your will find 16 of 254 pages following from this book -please enjoy them. I hope to publish the complete book along with the other 140 pages soon.

Tales of the Toltek re-Told

of Azatlan.

The Oracle.

									A
									B
									C
									D
									E
									F
									G
									H
									g.

1 2 3 4 5 6 7 8 9

"Ancient Translation"

ΔΙΥΩS AGATΛΑΥ ΚΕΙΟ η Σωιθ ΠΥΥΓ
ΚΑΙ ΓΙΕΦ ΑΥΙΜΙΟΥ ΚΙΥ Νξ ΙΙSΚΑ ηΠΥΥΓ
ΓΟΒΑΙΙξ η ΚΥΦΙΑΩΥ Κξηο ηξ ΗΕΑ-ΔΡξ
ΓΟξΦΟΙS οξ ΡΙΟΕΙ ┼┼┼ξ ΕΥ ΝΙΥΩS η ΝΝξ.

English Translation

Azatlan City, first cradle of the Gods:
Name of the Angels, before the great flood
Hope of the righteous, faith of Hea-D
Resting at last in ┼┼┼ξ (the City of the

Repeat the first part of last line three times

Excerpt from The Stone Book
page 3 of 256

Excerpt from The Stone Book
page 78 of 256

"The Giant of the Stones."

The Man,   Spiritual
Of figures   or ideal
holding the   order of Gods
sun moon & stars   Commanding
giving light   the elements
to the world   the Architect
the guide   of the universe
of mankind   the everlasting
                                                Containing all.

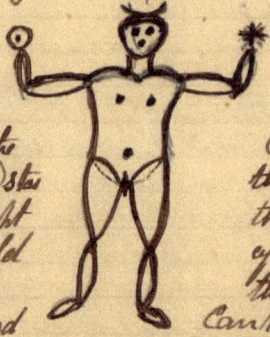

This Remarcable figure Consists of 32 figures
namely (1 2 3 4 5 6 7 8 9) the child gets
= (4 3 2 3 7 2 5 2 1) the no of each
there are no less than 10 pairs of Sixes.
with 2 Single Six and 2 eights = 16. thus
the figure is called "the Mistry of Six"
for Seven ths 7 of which there are 5×7 = 35
= 15 = 6. hence the No of Man is 66 © 6.
there are also ∵ ∴ making 6 points =
the total Sum added up is 138. total of Single
figures 32 = 6. and 1+3+8's = 12. or two Sixes.
is it any wonder that the early christians. Sel-
ected this figure as their ideal emblem of
their faith; their Crist on the Cross, that came
down from heaven, the ☉ of the ✳ (and the ☽ holy Ghost

at the base of the high and wild outer mountain
many colonies of the Talteks or the white people
Settled here as their land was not so fertile.
and after a time a new race of mixed blood
arose. and they entered into a covenant with
with the other four races. this is called the
"Everlasting Covenant" or the very long lasting covenant
by this time the Talteks had become efficient
in many arts and in particular in boat building
and fishing, — Three brothers one day out
fishing. discovered a shoal of small fish.
which they followed into a great cave. which
was made light by the fish. there was a strong
current outward, the boat was carried along
emerging at last into an open sea. on the
right of this sea they found a beautiful and
fertile land, after exploring the country
for a year, they followed a shoal of the same
fish. Setting current then running towards Azatlan
where they safely arrived — and informed the
different tribes of their wonderful discovery
the result was a new covenant, in which
it is Stipulated, that the three brothers
who discovered the Golden land or new world
and the Secret to and from Ancient Azatlan
they and they alone and their descendents are
appointed to conduct passengers to or from Azatlan

Excerpt from The Stone Book
page 5 of 256

Excerpt from The Stone Book
page 6 of 256

also, that the land between the sea and the mountain up to the top of the mountains shall be exclusively reserved to the Taltecs and the other Tribes shall settle beand to the westward, in the same order as in Azattan. a new Covenant was entered into, in the new country, that Branch of the Taltec family—descendants of the three discoverers, were called "Nergal" (Heavens founders or discoverers—in the course of time, the Nergals became aware that the sea was gaining on the land, or else the land was sinking. they sent messengers to warn the other settlements, advising them to build ships, and place their effect in them when the flood came, the Nergals were separated, because of the mountain barier between the settlements west of the mountains found refuge in the islands and eastern Asia. here to their great surprise they found other tribes or nations of whome they had no previous knowledge. these were Superstitious, offering human-Sacrifices, to their many gods, they were also Canibals, and ignorant of arts or sciences. as there were three different complection among the new Comers they were Called "Indian" meaning "the three first" the Indian entered into a Covenant, with the tribes they found in Asia &c.

Because of the superior knowledge of the Druids
they were to act as ministers of state and religion.
and teacher of the young.— &c to atend the
sacrifices both public and private &c c
they were to be free from paying taxes, or serving
in war, and to be royal in all things—
these Druidians and the different people of the
Covenant continued to follow the Sun to the
west. until they arrived at the shaws of the Med—
iteranean sea. here they discovered their long
lost friends the Neigals. of the Golden land.
who related to them their perigrinations since
the flood,— "When the flood came. most of the
people entered their Ships, but many were
caught in the mountains. the tops of which be—
came Islands. the Ships sailed Eastward
towards the rising Sun. they landed at the
first land (now called America) they came to.
here they settled on the table land mostly.
and built many cities. descending to the
sea towards the east (Gulph of mexico now)
they built ships and sailed eastward "on the
ocean rives (Gulph stheeme) to BEξίελ Ταφῶ
which they named "ΓΛΑΣ ΗΕξελιν." meaning
"the Blue-Sea-men" men of gigantic stature
and whose hair was blue! and the Beards.
these people were only found in one Island about
the center of the slowh (now called British Isles.

Excerpt from The Stone Book
page 7 of 256

Excerpt from The Stone Book
page 249 of 256

in another part of the county, and not wishing to take
the Stone away at the time, I made a facsimile of
the Characters. and noted the dimensions of the several
parts of the Stone, — this was in the year 1842 A.D.
Six years after this in 1848. I discovered another
Stone in the ruins of an old church undermined
by the sea. of which I also took a copy, which I
have since discovered to be the "Ogham a"
once common enough in the British Isles.
again in the year 1887. I made a third discovery,
in the heart of a very large fir tree, which was at
least 7 or 8 hundred years old. this time the Characters
were in a sheet of the gum at the 180th ring!
It so happened that in the year 1846 I joined two gent
lemen, for the purpose of exploring in north America
more particularly in Mexico. before starting my
guardian, presented me with a small charm.
under a promish not to look into it, while the
giver lived. unless under certain circumstances
and if I did see the contents, I must destroy the original, as soon as I translated the secret in
this I readily promished from regard to the giver.
rather than any benefit that I expected from it. —
It turned out however that there was enclosed
in the charm, "a Key" to these hieroglyphies !!!
and for the last nine years, I devoted all my time
to the study and Translation, of these ancient
secret Inspiration, and Revelation.

And having divided these into Lessons, which
may be had Singly, that is the translations, or if
all the Lessons are taken the Facsimile go with them.
The following is the List and the Price of each Lesson
1st A Table of the Dominical day, and Leap years.
or the day of the week Corresponding to any date. in
the Past - Present - or Future, Price
also written instruction, or verbal Price
2d Table of the Epacts of Centuries, & odd years.
or the age of the Moon on the 1st of any month from 5400.
to 2200 A.D. Price   Instruction. Price
3d Table of the Eclipses of Sun. or Moon. for any
year. (for 500 years - including the present Century) two
Examples of 113 years difference in date Price
Printed instruction, or verbal explanation Price
4th The perpetual Harascope, gives the true place of
the ☉ ☽ ✳ & the ⊕ on any hour of the day in any year.
also the hour of the day and month & year Price
the printed instruction on the same as verbal, Price
of the four Lessons are taken, the Facsimile will be
included, without instruction, instruction may
be had on certain Condition, (by Inspiration. &c)
        Rules of Inspiration and Revelation
1st Unit of multiplication, of the five genders ✳
2d the Select gender, Masculine and Feminine to be x by 5
to be x by any Single figure, Neuter to add 1 figure
3d The perpetual Triad of Generations, forward or backward
and the great Key of the Fathers (Saturn)

Excerpt from The Stone Book
page 250 of 256

Excerpt from The Stone Book
page 251 of 256

th The Tetra-grammaton words of many meanings.
th the Migrating tribe, and place (Decimal System)
th The figurative man — (Picture and Scroll writing)
th The Secret Alphabet, and Common alphabet (Greek)
th The Seal of the covenant of the Der-Krisdian)
Each Rule, with printed instruction Price   Each
if all the Rules are taken the Book of Primes and
Fractions will be included in the Set.
These are the most important, and if any of these rules
are allready known to the Student, one of the auxilia-
ry Lessons may be chosen in place of such Rule.

Auxilliary Lessons
1st The Taleisfeiries (Druid's Easter Money)
2d the Ogham. writing (maen hir)
3d The Scandinavian Runes (Futhark)
4th The original Alphabet (the Bardic harman) th Greek Roots
5th Ancient Zeological maps, and pictorial writing.
6th Poetical translation — the Book of Job of old.
or any of the other interesting Subject, such as the
First Christian Sermon on record. — Julius —
Caesar's account of the Druids. — A dress of the last
Arch Druid (in Britain) and many Scientific treatise

Rule for proving Tables of Dom Day
1600 = 7 (h) 1700 = 5 (7) 1800 = 3 (8) 1900 = 1 (0) so every
the years 28. 56 & 84. = the Century preceding; Subtract the
equal years from the odd years, if more than 28 but
if odd years are less count as remainder. the Months =
8 = 0   # ME   W N = 4. ⊃ = 5. ⊓ = 6. More
W = 1. 2. 3.

"Taleis ferries"

Arian—Dêr ▭ or ▭ Druid's Money.

The fac simile shaws bath Side of the Cain or Charm
these were made of gold, or Silver. and same time
of baser Mettle, or ather materials, they were warn as
Charms, and Supased to protect the wearer fram
evil influence. and as a mater of fact did so to
a certain extent. inasmuch that if the Passessar
Could read the Characters an them! he ashe must
be a member of the order of the Druids. fram
whame help would he had when in need; or ane
belanging to Same order in Cavenant with. them
if able to Letter ar devide the ward, Shawn an the ☉ face
one would ask. will yau Letter, or devide the ward? ?
the ather would answer, with yaur help I will do so.
"begin then" No yau begin, "No begin yau" Naw
Suppasing that ane was a Christian (af the Cavenant,
he would use five letter begining at either star * = *
I E H Z H. — A I Γ Θ E. (i̯e̯ ê̯ z̯ ê̯ — Ai g̯ª th̯ e) after
the ward was praperly given. the question would be asked
have yau any ather ward that I may better understand.
the ather would Say ⌂ Σ P ‖ Π ≡ ⌐∫ R P W̄ H ⌂
(this was dane by changing the right hand letter af each pair
fram the 1st to the 2nd devisian of the alphabet Greek)
what is that equal to? to him that Sits an the right
hand of the Haly ane! — I shall naw praceed
to explain the wanderful Candensatian of the Hieraglyphics

Excerpt from The Stone Book
page 135 of 256

Excerpt from The Stone Book
page 136 of 256

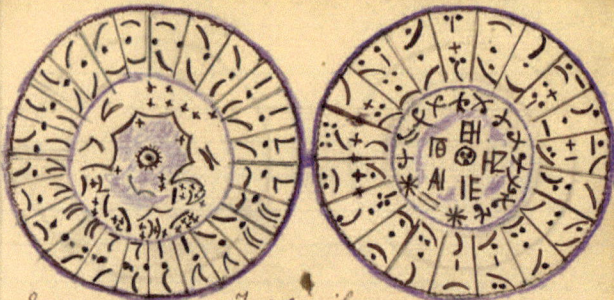

Sun.   Facsimile.   moon.

on the moon face there are five circles, the outer three
are devided into 19 equal spaces. each space to be
brought Horisontaly on the left of the moon ☉. the
outer circle is that of the Centuries, the 2ᵈ = + − ∝ =
the 3ᵈ is the Epact of the Century. the 4ᵗʰ circle is that
of the twelve months of the year shewing the number to
be added to the Epact for the age of the ☽ on the 1ˢᵗ of —
the iner circle of ten letters, are read as they stand (above)
the two outer circles on the Sun face are ÷
into 24 = parts. equal to the 24ʰ of the day or 15° or
2 weeks, the outer circle = the 12 Signs of the zodiac.
the iner circle = the 12 months of the year. both of
which are read on top, the 28 dots deviding them
shews the daily motion of the ☽. — the Hieroglyphics
in the middle and the arch (☉) of the Sun. must be
read as Stationary. (as above) the Stars below the arch
represent the milky way (via lacta) and the 7 Stars above
is the Sign of the great Bear (Ursa major) shewing the hours
of the day as well as the months and the years ~~~

A boomerang nevertheless of little use to us unless to play a tune on the "Ogham" Alphabet which you may do up or down as the whim takes you I shall give here a translation of another stone which I found in the ruins of an ancient Church that had been partly undermined by the sea (about 1848–9) of which I took a copy of at that time and which is evidently the same kind of writing as the Kerry Stones, but a little more elaborate — Many years after I accidentally discovered a "Key" to this Ogham Stone, after a while I was able to read it as well as if written in common figures or letters, and I am prepared to prove, to the satisfaction of any unprejudiced person, that it is a self-evident requiring no further proof than it contains There are three Colums, at the top of the first Colum is shown the full moon (☺) and near the bottom in the middle of the six crosses is the (☺) Sum this Colum is the common cycle of the Epacts the Middle Colum contains the Centuries from the Century 5400 old style or century before Anno Domini to the end of the 22 century of A.D. the purpose of it is to discover the age of the Moon at any time during these centuries, this it will do, by the average of time and will never be more than one day out which is owing to certain irregularity in the Motion.

Excerpt from The Stone Book
page 61 of 256

Excerpt from The Stone Book
page 62 of 256

The Alphabet.

1	2	3	4	5	6	7	8	9	10

11	12	13	14	15	16	17	18	19	20

Oghama 3

> = one ten. ⌇ = two tens.
these were notches on the edge.
⌇ = 30 or nothing in Epacts.
The right hand Column
is the rule to find the Century.
Start with the middle Cross
at the foot, Count five ⇊↓
thrice, and Six ↖↑ once.
when the foot is reached Start
again at the top, or vis versa
the mouth on the left margin
as shewn here was not on the
original Stone. neither the
alphabet, as given here.
Observe, the Cyphers are
not given for 1800 = 18 = ⌇
Opposite this in first Column
Stands 1111 or 1111 Epact.
of that Century, & the 5 = years.
Count downward one Epact for each year in excess
the Epact thus found will be the Epact of the year
to represent add the number of the Epact opposite but
not counting the tens > = age of the) in the first.

Maen lia. Stone

"The original Alphabet"

A B Γ Δ E Z H Θ I K Λ M N
1 2 3 4 5 6 7 8 9 10 11 12 13

Ξ O B P Σ T Y Φ X Ψ Ω
14 15 16 17 18 19 20 21 22 23 24

The Capital Letters of the greek Alphabet is a Copy of this alphabet. using straight lines instead of the serny circle, inasmuch as this alphabet as shewn by the Stone records, is older than the Greek Nation, and it is known that the Greeks used another alphabet before adopting this. & it is evident that each of these letters are underlined wards and in some at least they adopted the ward as the name of the letter, without translating it. & it must be borne in mind, that this alphabet is represented by one single character in the in the Neſal alphabet, or by a single figure and the sign of Parcession, I shall give a facsimile. of this kind which I found in a Cave over the stone of entrance into an inner chamber. there are 40 characters in 40 syllables and every one is a vowel, that is independant sound that is sounded by one impulse of the Voice without the aid of another sound (as the Consonant) I shall also give the equivilants in plain figures and also the same in greek letter (for sound) with a literal translation of the same in English.

Excerpt from The Stone Book
page 69 of 256

Excerpt from The Stone Book
page 70 of 256

∧ "Garsin Garddewin" (Taliesin)

[Facsimile of hieroglyphic characters]

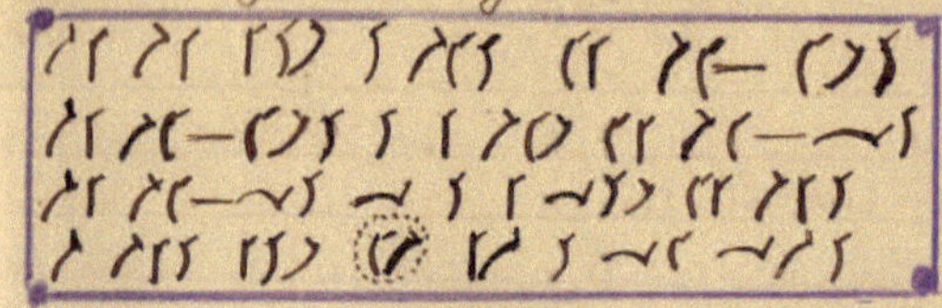

Facsimile of the Hieroglyphics

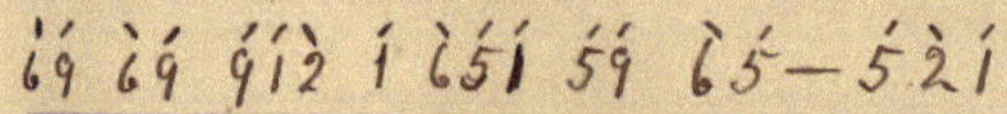

[Row of symbols]

Sign of Res minutes

Οι Ὥι Ιαυ α Ὥὲα ει Ὥὲ — Ευα
Οι Ὥὲ—Ευα α ι Ὥὲυ ει Ὥὲ—ῆᾶ
Οι Ὥὲ—ῆᾶ η α ι ῆαυ ει ωια
Ο ωια Ιαυ (ὲὥ) Ιο (α) ῆε ῆοα

Greek text

From his egg Jave weaves his winter-web
From his winter-web he gaes weaves his Summer-web
From his Summer-web he gaes to seed his eggs
From Jave's eggs is Jo·b· Hê (and) Hoa

Translation

Observation— The word "gar-sin, garthewin"
is subject to a dispute among interpreters.
the first part gor. means superior; a extreme.
by the Dictionary—Sin. means Donation; Alms.
but in the book of Ezekiel 41 ch 16 v "Garsigan"
means in the English Version Door-Post. now
it strikes me, that the form of the Hieroglyphics
which is that of the crecent moon, more particularly
so, since the ancient name of the moon was "Sin"
(Chaldean)

The root of the matter

	Branch	365850Y another hidd	593		
*503			593		
725			716		
565			466		
*509	599		418		
185	176		283		
523	424		704		
743	652		637		
763	861		303		
781	962		723		
949	873		745		
162	701	791	583		
865	907	988	707		
512	369	261	367		
824	147	956	327		
656	307	414	381		
411	363	643	975		
913	777	762	522		
738	340	871	833		
214	129	971	755		
641	109	972	502	592	
942	181	882	815	806	
855	973	800	557	458	
*503	702		320	229	
725	817			110	
565	377				
*509	336				
Prime	480	Branch of the Branch	Prime Twin 593 of 503	Branch of the Twin	

The No 503 and 593 = ↑ are called the Twins because ↑ upwards hath Produce the same 855. but ↓ downwards are entirely different, yet all the roats, will all end in the product of the Twins. The roats are supposed to end when the right hand figure becomes a cypher and to Branch out when a cypher is the figure placed in the middle or 9 which is its Twin.

Starting from 503 ↓↑ up or down, the cycle = 22 generation from 503 to 949 is 14 generation Read and from 725 ↓ 9 gen. ↑↓ mean opposite direction ↑ ··· = (unit) & figure of Parent figure

Excerpt from The Stone Book
page 103 of 256

The original manuscript of

"The Three Mermaids"

The Three Mermaids.

In the year 1800. at a gay Ladys school in the west of England three young Ladys heretofore Strangers to each other, became fast friends, their names in full were, May Mortimer de St. John, May Tremanmaur gary. & May Morvrin Evans. the first was a native of the west of France (Britage) the 2nd of the west of England (Cornwal) and the third from the west coast of Wales. the curious part about them is that their names are nearly of the same literal meaning. John, gary, & Evans. all mean young. and the second name Mortimer—(sea of the house of Mer — Mercury) Treman maur (môr) House of man — Place, of the Sea. Morvrin (sea of the hill — mount) and because of this reference to the Sea, doubtless, they received the name of Mermaids. when I was a boy the three resided in Cornwal, and once every year they (with others) visited a famous Stone Circle, and a certain Cave & Relics. observing some Ceremonies, the object and nature of which at that time was unknown to me. particularly the one on the sea-shore. in which I always appeared as having the chief part to play. I was taught to say a number of verses in a language unknown to me then, but which I have lately discovered what it was. or partly so at least. M. M. E. married one Captain Robart. a native of Cornwal. the other two as far as I know were never married. the eldest son of Captn R. also became a Captain & part owner of the ship — I was taught, and believed, that he was my Father. but recently I have discovered. that he had saved me when a baby not a month old. from the shipwreck of his ship. on bard of which I had been since the 2nd or 3rd day after my birth — and he had adopted me as his son my own Parents having been lost in the shipwreck. whoever they were. If I had only even suspected, these particulars. when I was young. or any of these "three mermaids" alive I might have discovered the secret

THE THREE MERMAIDS

In the Year 1800 at a young Ladys school in the West of England three young Ladys, heretofore Strangers to each others, became fast friends, their names in full were Mary Mortimer de St John, Mary Temanmaur Young and Mary Morvrin Evans. The first was a native of the west of France (Brittany), the 2nd, of the west of England (Cornwal), and the third from the west coast of Wales.

The curious part about them is that their names are nearly the same Literal meaning: John, Young and Evans all mean young, and the second name, Mortimer, sea of the house of Mer-Mercury

Teman Maur (Mar), house of Man-
Place of the sea, Morvren (Sea
of the hill- Maunt) and because
of this Reference to the Sea, doubtless, they Received the name of
MERMAIDS. When I was a boy
the three Resided in Cornwal, and
once every year they (with others)
visited a famous stone circle and
a certain cave & Relics, observing
some ceremonies, the object

and nature of which at
that time was unknown to me,
particularly the one on the sea-
shore, in which I allways appeard
as having the Chief Part to play.
I was taught to say a number
of verses

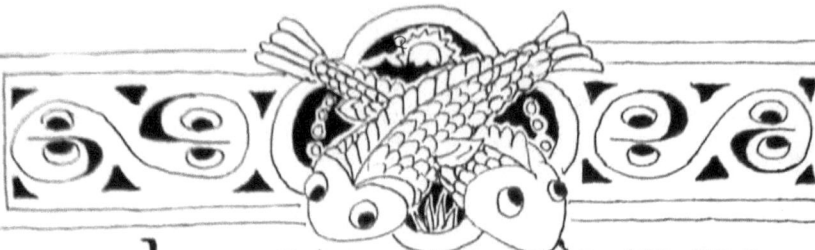

in a language unknown to me then, but which I have lately discovered what it was, or partially so, at least. Mary Morvrin Evans married one Captain Robarts, a native of Cornwal. The other two as far as I know, were never marid. The oldest son of Captain Robarts also became a Captain and part owner of the ship ___. I was taught, and believed, that he was my Father. But recently I have discovered that he had saved me when a baby not a month old from the shipwreck of his ship, on bord of which I had been since the 2nd or 3rd day after my birth ~ and he had

adopted me as his son, my own parents having been lost in the ship-wreck, whoever they were. If I had only even suspected these parti-culars, when I was young, and any of these 'three mermaids' alive, I might have discovered the secret.

But the three are long since gone to kindred spirits. The first to go was my reputed grandmother, when I was about six years old. On this occasion I was the Chief mourner (according to Custom). Very strange indeed were the circumstances in connection with the funeral.

But as theese belongs properly to the next number of 'the Translator', I shall confine myself for the present to a strange discovery I did make while the two were yet alive... Aunt Mortimer ...and Aunt Young. At the time I had no suspicion theese two had any hand in the discovery but I shall give them the benefit of the doubt I entertain at present. It was the discovry of the 'STONE BOOK' one of the most remarcable books ever written by man. By man I do not mean one man, for hundreds of men have

written this book, but all of it
is after the same Rule, or maner.
Allthough there are three
distinct Periods and each have
their distinctive character,
again, if I had had any idea
about the contents of this
Book, at the time, I might
have coppyed such parts that
would be most interesting to
the Reader and myself. What
I actually did coppy are not
lacking in interest, however ~
they shall appear in future num-
bers. Unless I shall be for-
tunate enough to be able to
take a facsimile of all of the

First trip to Wales

One of the main reasons for this journey
was to see Dr. David Davies 'the wee person' I had
met in Pasedena in 1979 who I had felt had been
instrumental in my decision to study the Druids.
I had not communicated in more than a year but
he wrote me a letter September 10th and a 2nd
letter soon after that which is quoted below:

"The backgound story you give in your letter is
most interesting. As you say, Pasedena produced
the catalyst – not by accident. The sequence of
events is typical of a planned campaign, in which
the initiative belong to a different "dimension". To
ensure the success of the project it was essential that
I should not be available until you had already con-
tacted the "Ancient" with an Egyptian-Oriental
face. These are two corners of a 'triangle', the 3rd is
Druidic. To refer to the complete Triangle, I some-
times use the term DRAVIDIAN, a word which takes
us back far beyond the recorded "history" or story
of prehistoric man. Intuitive-mind can hear the
voice of INTUITION as it reads the AKASHIC
RECORDS , but the rational mind has to bring
IMAGINATION into action in order to even attempt
to express the EXPERIENCE in words. Those papers
were destined to come into your hand, but only
after you had already been prepared by the YOU-
WITHIN to be ready to handle them.."

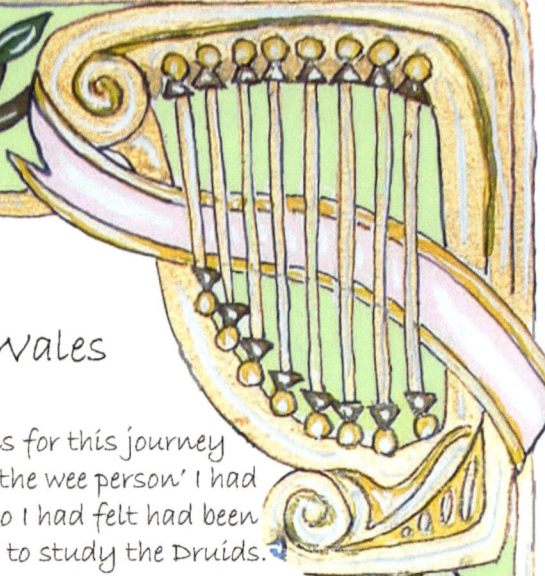

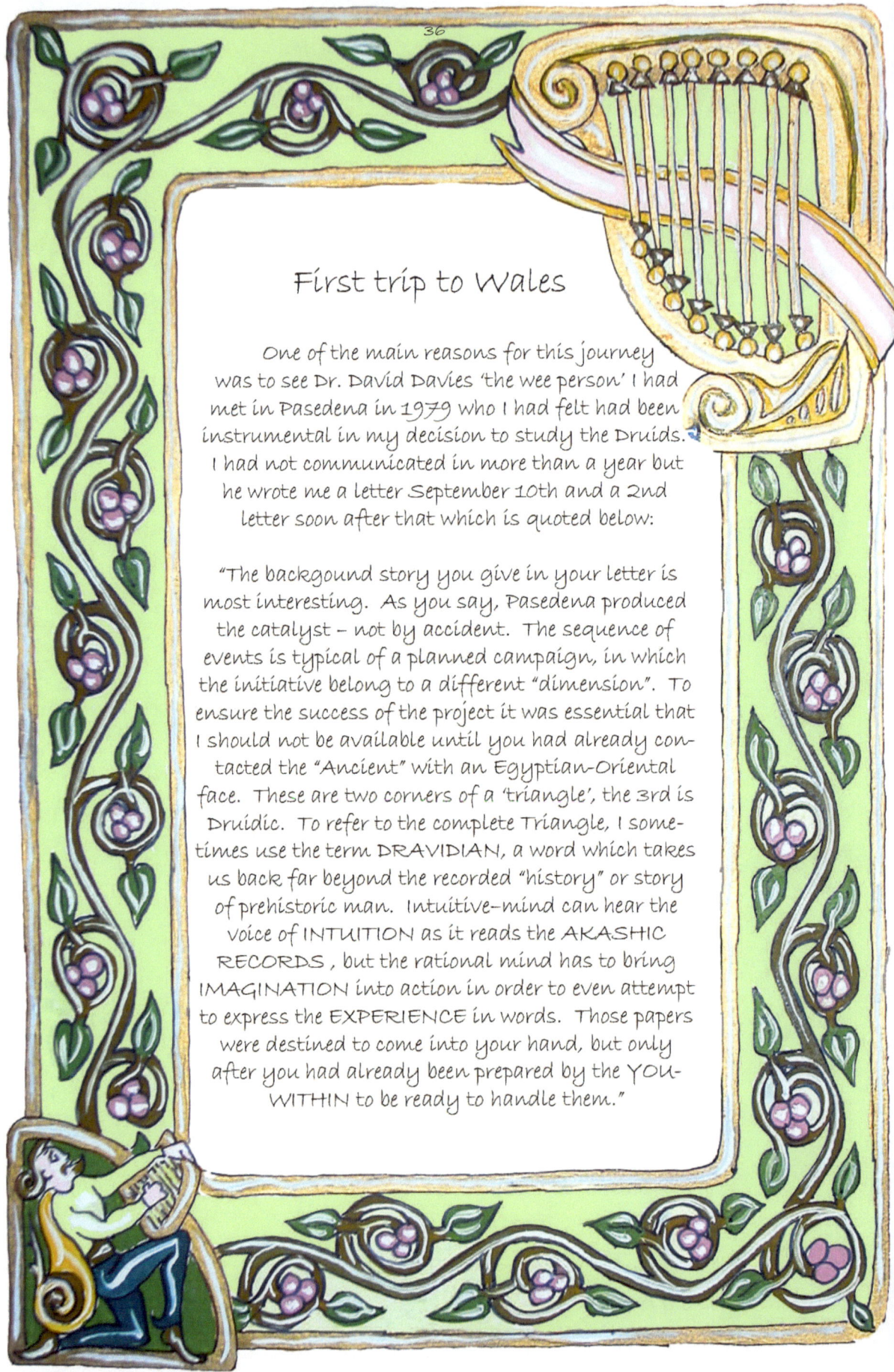

Dr. David Davies Letters-
(great motivation for me)

After writing to Dr. David Davies I received
another letter which read:
"Our thanks for your letter and for the news that
you have many projects in hand, ranging from the
Druidic past to the children's work on nutrition
and health. The sequence of events in getting the
papers is wonderfully monitored: it has a dramatic
quality about it, e.g. the Druidic impulse after
Pasedena, the unexpected possession of the papers
with all the written trimmings to provide the back-
ground for any detailed study, and then getting
the paintings and sketches by Tomtu Huron
Roberts, J.H.R.'s son. The two of you are ideally
matched to the task of both the papers and paintings. We wish you success with the Exhibition in
Vancouver in April and May. You are wise to give
yourself seven years to tackle the J.H.R. papers. It
will take quite a long time to check the contents of
the papers and to carry out adequate research into
the ideas present. By the time you could probably
have sufficient material for a kind of religio-phili-
sophical documentay book as well as an inspiration novel. By that time it will have led you
through many experiences, which will themselves
reveal great depths of meaning even in what you
had apparently thoroughly mastered. The challenge is there; it is the challenge to sit in the
"empty seat" (the Siege Perilous) at Arthur's round
Table, the CATHEDRA OF INTUITION."

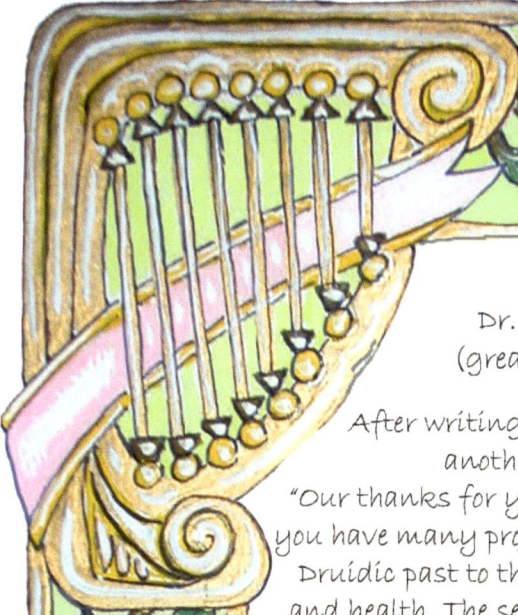

On my second journey to Wales I arrived
at Heathrow with my over- the -
shoulder bag and one suitcase with my
new Native American peace pipe given to
me by a special shaman, my healing crystal
my eagle feathers and assorted clothing and
I passed through customs and immigration with
my water stained passport showing the likeness
of Grizzly Adams staring back at their robot faces I
quickly found the bus to Redding and then a train
to Cardiff. Bill Meilan a professor in Edmonton, also
a Welsh bard had given me the name of a number of
people to contact. In Cardiff I found the phone number
of Dr. David Davies but no one was at home and won-
dered if it was the right number. I made the decision
to go to the National Library in Aberystwyth. The
following morning I went and met Mr. De.E.
Williams, assistant keeper – Dept of MSS and
records, the person Bill Meilan recommended. He was
most excited when I supplied him with a geneology of
John Hugh Roberts as shown in his dairies. I was
advised that the Roberts manuscripts seem to be a
totally different source as that of Iolo Morganweg's
writings from the early 19th century. From here I left
for Abergavanney to meet with David Davies.
I met Dr. Davies and told him the story about the
Stone Books and his conscious or unconscious involve-
ment in contributing to my destiny in receiving
them. I always thought of him as one of the 'wee
people" and found out, he was in fact only 4"10" and
90 pounds, although being in his presence one felt his
immense power. The next couple of days were a
delight.

That evening, and thirteen hours the following day and two hours Thursday morning we sat opposite each other comfortable in our armchairs talking on the many channeled tangents of our minds.

It was of great inner pleasure to sit with this man of letters - a 82 year old professor Emeritus. We touched upon many wonderful topics not the least were Druidical presences and teachings direct from the ancients.

Meeting Everild Helweg Larson-Young

David had arranged for me to stay with a "Fellow" of the Royal Geogaphic Socity, Everild Helweg-Larson-Young , a dynamic 74 year lady who was an explorer in the 30'sthrough to the 60's in South America, Easter Island, Galapagous Island and China. She traveled these countries, not as a tourist in the cities, but as a explorer traveling the backwaters and checking out old ruins and old myths. She has a number of books to her credit that relate to her adventures in these countries. So each day I spent talking to David and each night until midnight I would listen to stories of exploring the high Andes with Everild, by the time I fell asleep I was super saturated with mystical adventures. David in one of his previous lives had been a "Druid priest" of some stature living in a cave in this mountain - Skyrrid or Holy Mountain. (This story was from some writings from another professor Emeritus and friend of Davids) and it was then that I decided this was the mountain I was to climb to do my pipe. The new sacred pipe I had beem given was a mountain pipe.

A Trek up the Holy Mountain

David was to drive me to the foot of the mountain. I was to climb and be back by 1 to go to lunch with Everild. The last I would see David on this trip would be at the foot of the mountain. I got out as David turned his Morris Minor around in a small turn-about. He pulled the car up to a stop opposite me in the road and, even though sitting on a 5" foam rubber he pad had problems comfortably fitting the car, shouted out" Dale, there's one last word," and with his arm extending striaght up out of the window and with a knowing eye penetrating my person he shouted "Excalibre" and off he drove. I turned filled with a new purpose, stepped over the fence and made my way up the path, after first accepting a black raven feather directly in my path, to make my way to the top of Skyrrid. I was looking for a cave of the Druid priest from so long ago. I found a small bounlder and noticed a deep rather large hole beside it and somehow felt it might have been overtop of the original cave. So be it, it felt good and right to do the pipe there...as I extended the pipe up into the sky, facing east which meant facing into the mountain, there was a loud roaring sound behind me and as I turned my head - a jet with a helmeted pilot facing towards me was easily visible thundered past. He was 30 feet below and 500 ft out from me and I hope he, in that split second, saw the image of me holding the mountain pipe extended to the heavens and hopefully it is imprinted somewhere in the abyss of his mind.

Letter from the National Library
of Wales 1981

Dear Professor Meilan,

It was a great pleasure to meet you last week. I am
only sorry our conversation had to be so short
because of my committee meeting. I am sure Mr.
Huws and Williams gave you all possible help.
The Roberts manuscript of which you told us is
fascinating and certainly worth transcribing and
analyzing fully. Its author seems to have pos-
sessed a zeal for recondite knowledge which was
not uncommon during the period. I know of no
other source which affords so clear a glimpse into
the mind of such a person. Any help we can give
with the process of transcribing and editing the
material we shall be glad to supply. And when
you have done with the manuscripts we should of
course be more than glad to offer it a permanent
home her, if its owner minded to give it to us.

Comment:
At a later date, in 1999, I had another meeting at
the National Library of Wales and they decided
they would like to look at the manuscripts to
appraise them for purchase. I really appreciated
the interest they showed but decided I needed them
around for the present, at least for inspiration and
for creating the quest journal which I knew one
day we would share.

In between I went to Criccieth and the first evening ventured down to the church and across the street to the antique shop called "The Forge". I had with me three original papers and the Stone Book of Knowledge.

I introduced myself to the proprietor, a Jim Young, asking about the availability of reference books about local history of Llaniestyn as it being the home of Roberts grandmother, one of the 3 mermaids. Well with rising enthusiasm Jim scanned the papers and commenced to give me various sources to follow-up for the Roberts story. He pulled one book a 1813 edition of History of Wales by Theophilus Evans, originally printed in 1740. He said with the slightest twinkle in his eye, that I should come to his house in Criccieth that evening as he might have a book or two I might be interested in on Druids and Bardic lore. Three days later still not having visited him at his home, I entered the shop and he grabbed me by the arm and said, "Come, I have to help my friend, who is doing some repair work on my home, and I want you to see my library". Well he lived in a beautiful house, one of 7 row houses, 4 stories high that bordered the beach in Criccieth which happens to look south over Sarn Badric and Black Rock Sands. He and his wife are the only inhabitants of this 12 room house. He led me though each room from the first floor. I marveled at the number of gold embossed leather bound books that lined the rooms & took up to two walls per room; stopping every so often and pulling out a 1650 edition of the Runes or 1777 edition of history of a certain Welsh parish etc. 'My heart had goose bumps on it'. Each time we entered a room he glanced quickly at my expression which by this time was quite imbecilic.

Finding Druid books and
the Grandmother's House

He could see, the shock of my reaction to this vast source of information, and I remember the sparkle and glimmer in his eyes as he glanced at me. As we went from room to room he told me how he started his collection on druids and early Celtic history. After the war he told of driving through the Welsh countryside picking up boxes of books left on the side of the roads by the people. In some areas of Wales it was frowned upon to have any books about Druids, Ancient Celts et. I eventually purchased a 1711 book on the Druids of Angelsy. I understand his collection has been dispersed the last few years. It really was one of those magical syncronistic moments for me on this trip.

I could not get a boat over to Bardsey Island but sat across from the burial ground of the 20,000 saints and the home of Merlin and did my pipe.

An important moment for my earlier trips to Wales was finding John Hugh Roberts grandmothers house. I was with Professer Jordan Paper and we went to the little town of Llaniestyn. It was hidden away and off the tourist track. I was pointed to a little stone house. I knocked on the door- It was answered by a very well rounded lady who when reading the geneology I had brought with me confirmed she was a distant relative of J.H. Roberts. I climbed the magical Carn Fadryn near the village which gave a wonderful panoramic view of the green hills all around and the waters of the Irish Sea and the sea covering the Land of Teman. The only sound was the wind and that of sheep baaing.

44

"THE GHELUERTH"

OR

BONFIRE AT HALLOWEEN

John Hugh Roberts wrote this paper about his
experience in Wales as a boy at
an important ceremony

45a

"The Gaelcerth" or Banfire at Halloween.

One of those Ceremonies that has survived since the time of
the Druids, is yet kept in Wales, on the 11th of November (+)
every year, or at least they were observed there during the time
that I was in that County (from 34 to 40) I took part in its Ceremonies,
and I am told they are yet (1855) kept up, for a week before the time it is
a busy time with the Children, and some old people too, gathering materials for this Banfire, which is lighted at Sunset, (old style 11th mostly)
anciently every house in the neighborhood put out their fires, so that
they may be relighted from the Gaelcerth, but in my time but few of
the old families did this, a discription of the last I attended then (1840)
with some slight local variation, will answer for all of them —
It was Wednesday (+) 11th of November (+) 1840, the moon yet looked full (17 old)
the Sun sett about 4:30, when I lit the Banfire, it was my right to do
so because I had gathered the greatest amount of materials for it, the master
of ceremony that night was a Stranger to me a very old man who sat
near the fire until the Signs, told him the time to sound the Trumpet!
the Sign of the Bear was low in the north thus ◡, the Plime or 1st star
(upper) of the Chair of Casiopea on the Zenith orian & the Pliades (and the D) in
the East. and the "Trybedh-y dri" — the Tribet, or Triad stars of the Druids
in the west with the Milky way nearly from east to west, then the old man
slowly arose and handed me the Trumpet, which I sounded, keeping
time with the Motions or Signs he made (I had done this before —)
while thus engaged there was a great Commotion among the large Crowd
"the Queen of the Fairies was aproaching, she was dressed so fantastically that
her best friend could not have known her — at her aproach a large ring
was formed, into which the Queen marched, with a number of her subjects —
the master of the Ceremonies aproached the ring and conversed with the Queen.

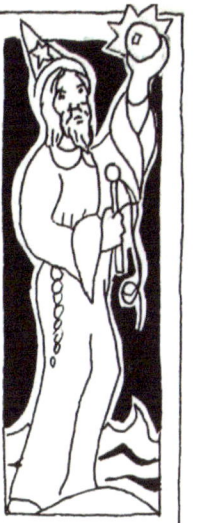

One of those cere-
monies that has sur-
vived since the time of the
Druids is yet kept in
Wales on the 11th of
November
evry year, or
at least they
were observed there
during the time that I
was in that country (from
'34 to '40). I took part in
the ceremonies and I am
told they are yet (1888)
kept up.

For a week before the time, it is a busy time with the children & some old people, too, gathering materials for this BONFIRE which is lighted at sunset (old style: 11th, mostly). Anciently, evry house in the neighborhood put out their fires so that they may be relighted from the GAELCERTH but in my time but five of the old families did this.

A description of the last I atended there (1840) will answer for all of them...

It was WEDNESDAY 11th of NOVEMBER, 1840. The moon yet looked full (17 day old). The sun set about 4:30 when I lit the Bonfire. It was my right to do so because I had gathered the greatest amount of materials for it.

The **Master of Ceremony** that night was a stranger to me, a very old man who sat near the fire untill the signs told him the time to sound the **TRUMPET**. The sign of the **BEAR** was low in the north, thus : ⌐J. The Prime, or 1st star (upper) of the **CHAIR** of **CASIOPEA**

on the ZENITH, ORION, the PLIADES & the (in the east, and the 'TRYBEDH·Y DRE', the TRIBAT, OR TRIAD stars of the DRUIDS in the west, with the Milky Way nearly from east to west. Then the old man slowly arose and handed me the Trumpet, which I sounded, keeping time with the motions or sounds he made.

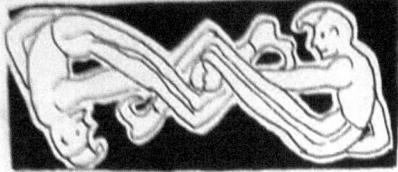

I had done this before~).

While thus engaged, there was a great comotion among the large crowd. The Queen of the FAIRIES was approaching. She was dressed so fantasticaly that her best friend could not have known her. At her aproach, a large ring was formed.

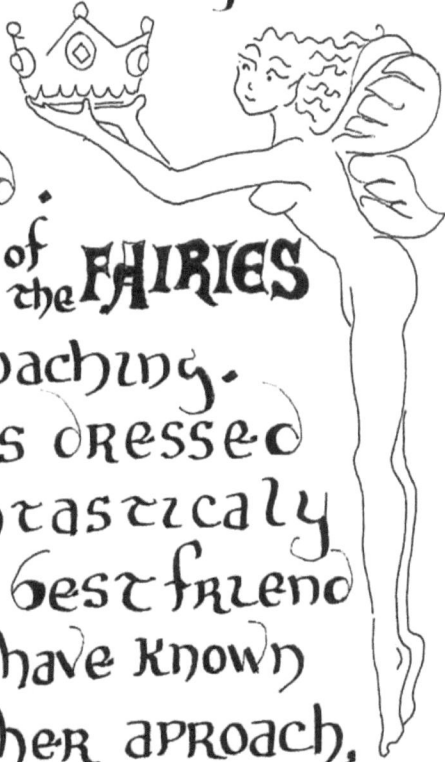

() :   "Nennius"   91.

This name appears to me more representative
than personal, addapted for a purpose
Nen, means that which is above us, as the
vaults of the skey — the roof of a house &c
a very appropriate name for a Bishop &c
and the Heaven of the Christian, as differing
from the ancient Druidical idea of it.
the dates 946, & 858 (given by Gale & Gunn &c &&&)
differ by 88 years. and counting 34 years as the age
of Christ at the Crusifixion he must have lived
54 years in Britain. it is remarcable that the
old style among the Druids ended with the Century
5400. and the new Style was Counted henceforth.
which has the same unit as the old Style. but
it is plain that the Present Anadomini does not
represent the Birth-Crusifixion or death of cht
but is simply an Astranomical arangement
The works of Nennius, proves beand a doubt
that the ancient Christians. that is the order of
Bishops, and such high christians were Members
of the order of the Druids and had access
to the Stone books of the ancient Neryds (Druids)
this is proved by the "Lispa Laupk" Purporting
to be a translation of a part-by same Rev ——

Original writings of Nennius
First page of a 4 page manuscript
outlining that he, Roberts discovered the
Bishop Nennius's bones.

Nennius

Bishop Nennius is stated as having
lived in North Wales in the late
8th & early 9th century, and
is identified as the author of
the Historia Brittonum.

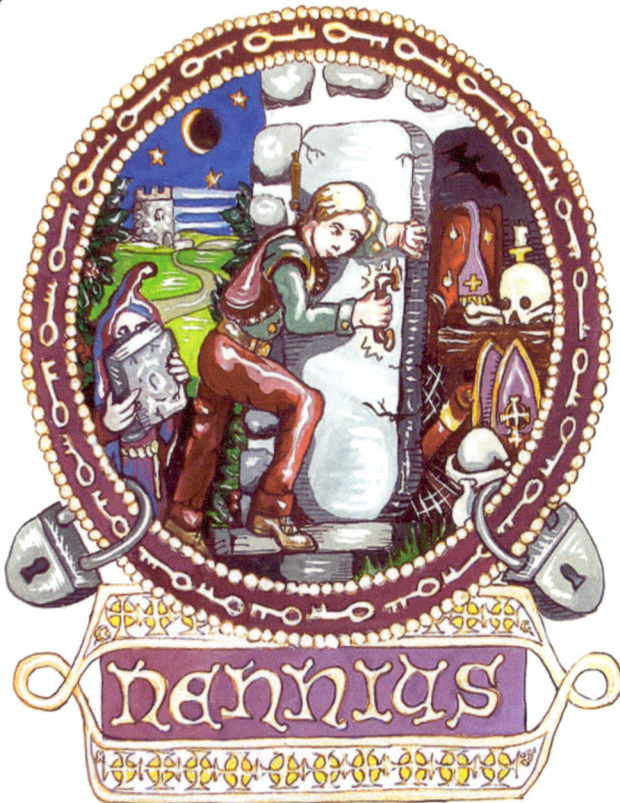

nannius

This name appears to be more representative than personal, ad-dobpted for a purpose. NEN means that which is above us as the vaults of the sky, the roof of a house, etc, a very apropriate name for a BISHOP etc.

and the Heaven of the Christian as differing from the ancient DRUIDICAL idea of it. The dates 946 & 858 (given by Gale + Gunn, as shown) differ by 88 years, and counting 34 year as the age of Christ

AT THE CRUCIFIGATION

The must have lived 54 years in Britain. It is remarcable that the old style among the **DRUIDS** ended with the **Century** 5400, and the new style was counted henceforth, which has the same unit as the old style. But it is plain that the present

ANO DOMINI

does not represent the Birth ~ Crucification or death

☧ or Chͬͭ ☧

but is simply an Astronomical arrangement. The works of NENNIUS proves beyond a doubt that the ancient CHRISTIANS

that is the order of BISHOPS, and such high dignitarys were members of the order of the DRUIDS and had access to the Stone books of the ancient NARGALS (DRUIDS). This is proved by the "LIRPA LAUPH" purporting to be a translation of a part~

by same Revᵈ.

Curious enough, this Reverend gentleman has put it on record in that book ~ the Curs that was to follow ~ a breach of the ancient covenant, which he was then and there violating. But he says he trusted in GOD and had no FEAR.

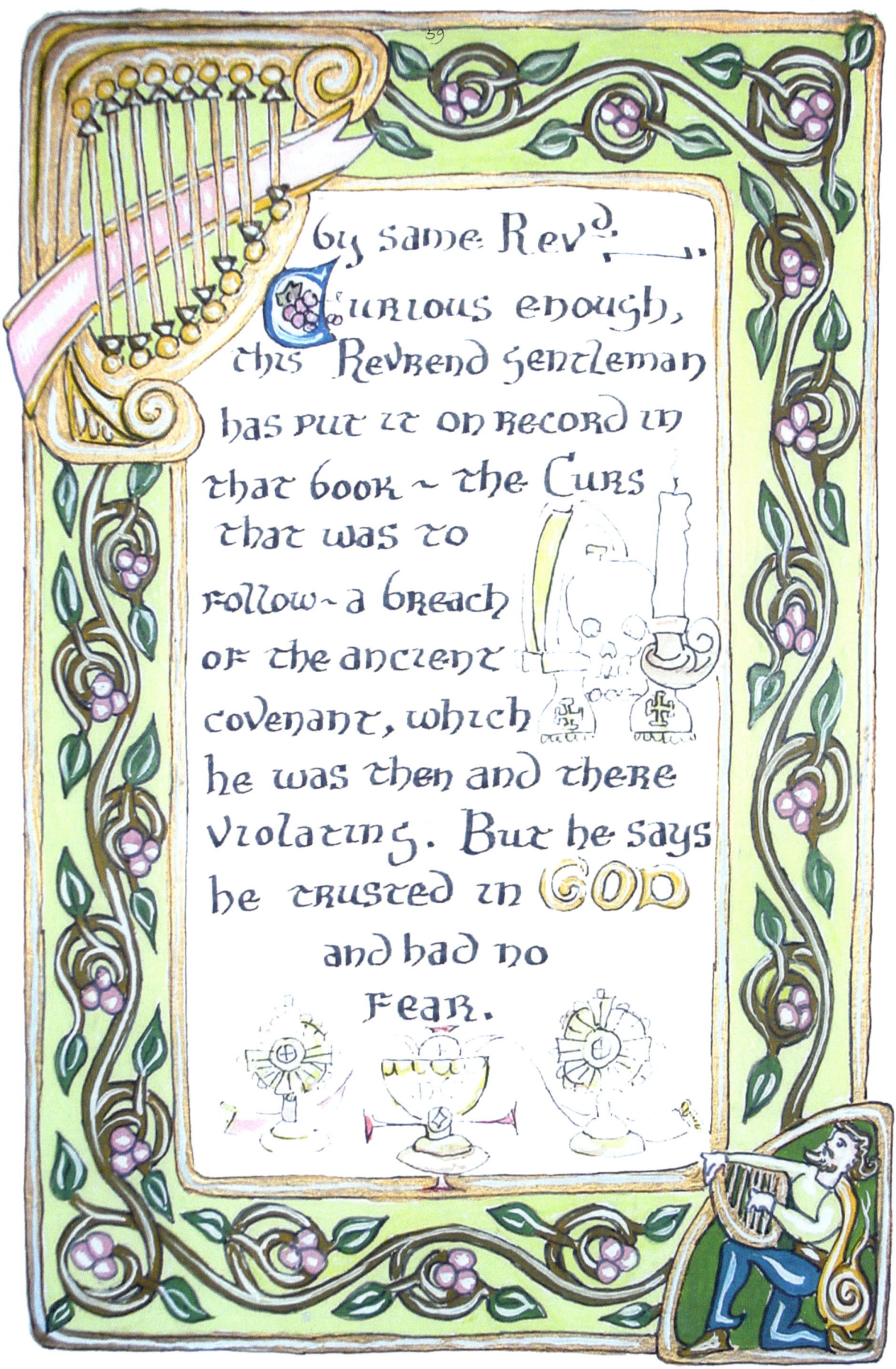

W hen I discovered this book in the underground chamber in that old mansion long ago, I gazed with wonder on his bones still partly in the stone chair wher he had pen'd thees words centuries ago. There were some tatters of his vestments also thare and other things proving that he was in 'HOLY ORDER'.

The cause of this man's death was his disregard of the key. Doubtless he thought it was only a superstitious observance, unworthy of a man who trusted in GOD.

SANCTUS

The maner of entering this chamber was through a stone door. There was some arrangments attached to this door, that by standing on another stone

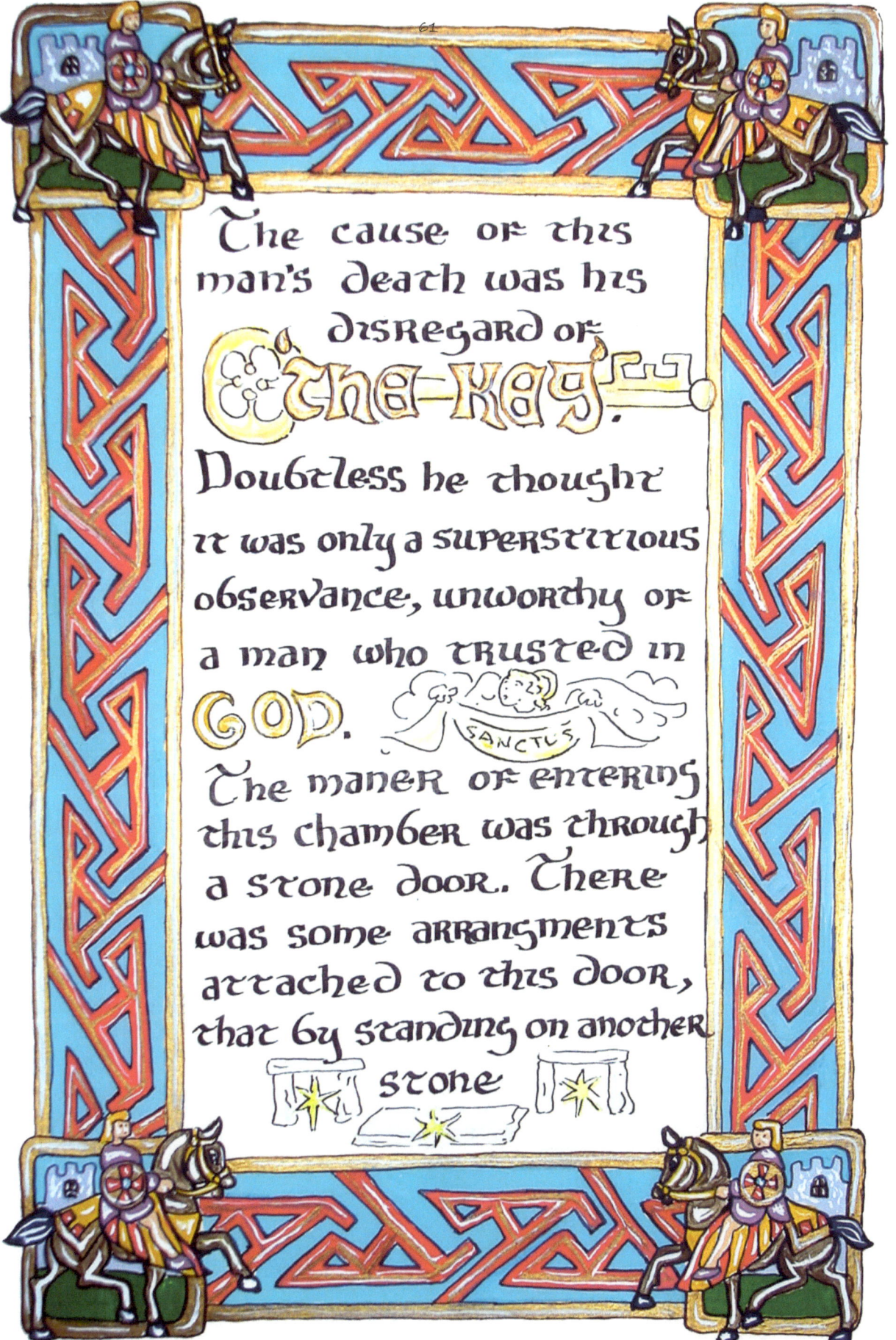

CHIEF FESTIVALS OF THE DRUIDS

Chief Festivals of the Druids
written in the 1880's by J.H. Roberts
Describing ceremonies he participated in
Wales and Cornwall in the 1830's - 40's

"Chief Festivals of the Druids"
The first on the list in respect to time, is "the Feast of the Red Swords" or the Red Stars — it is a movable feast like "Easter" it commemorates the first Covenant in Azatlan, which happened at the time of the full moon in the Sign Taurus (the Bull) and the Sun in Sign Scorpio (Scorpion) at the night flow of the waters (tide) three Brothers were fishing (Hea-Hoa-Hua) there appeared an immense number of fish, literally filling the waters. having filled the Boat during the night the fish suddenly disappeared. having followed the fish into a great Cave, they explored this Cave and came to a Subterranean River that came out on the other side of the mountains into a great open Sea or ocean this was a great discovery, inas much as the surplus population could be disposed of in Colonies as they became too numerous to dwell in Azatlan hence was founded the Covenant of Azatlan, some time called the ever-lasting Covenant, (sacrificial) the meaning of this word strictly is, Everlasting "as long as the Signs appear" the chief Sign is the Bull (Bula - in the Kymric) or Taurus. 8. the chief Star in this Sign is "Aldebaran" (Bull's eye) a ruddy Star. opposite to this star in the heavens is the other ruddy star "Antares" with the first is the full moon, and with the last the Sun, and mars the ruddy Planet. 8. is the correspondent, or warrior King, the movable star. allegorically the agent that executes the decrees of the three Kings (Orion) the three stars called the belt of Orion, are also called the three Kings representing three Tribes or nations in the Golden land or new Azatlan (Colonies) that is the Continent that then existed where now the Pacific ocean is — in the Islands of that ocean at the present day this feast is yet observed at the Fiji Islands the appearance of these fish or worms that make their appearance only on two days in the year first in October 6th and about the end of November (between 20th & 25th of the month) they appear in countless my-riads. for a few hours in the morning before the rising of the Sun. at the first appearance of the Sun they disappear and are not again seen until the next year. they call this feast of the great (innumber) "Balolo" (Palolo viridis) in Britain this feast was called "Gwyil-Bwlala" but as these fish are not found in Britain the "Lampreys" or sand eels is made to do duty, hence it's also called "Gwyil-Lymrien" (Lamprey's feast) is it not a strange coincidence, that the name of the star Antares (Anti-Ares) strongly

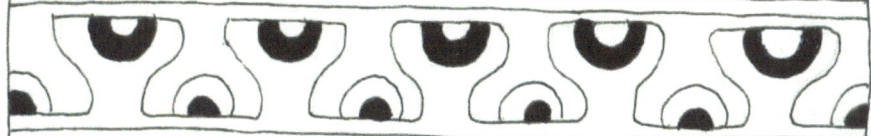

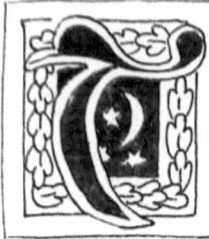

The first on the list in respect to time is 'The feast of the Red Swords' or the Red Stars. It is a movable feast like Easter. It commemorates the first Covenant in Azatlan which happened at the time of the full moon in the Sign Taurus (the Bull) and the Sun in Sign Scorpio (Scorpion) at the night flow of the waters (tide) Three Brothers were fishing (Hea, Hoa & Hua)... There appeared an immense number of fish

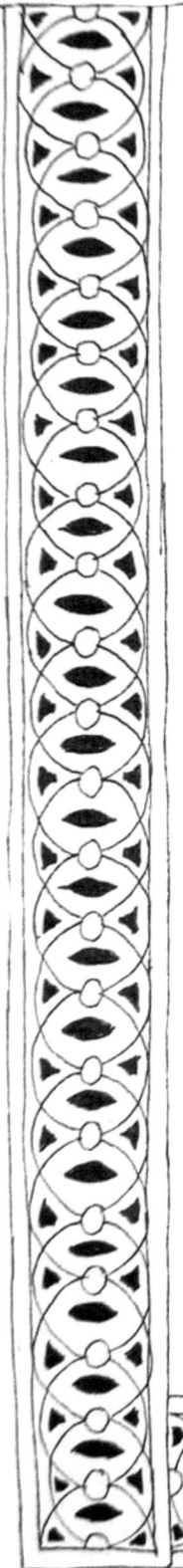

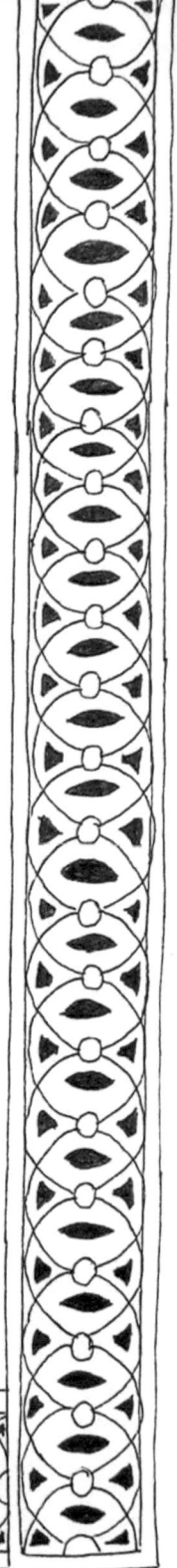

literally filling the waters.
Having filled the boat during
the night, the fish suddenly
disapeared. Having followed
the fish into a great cave
They explored this cave and
came to a subteranean river
that came out on the other
side of the mountains into
a great open sea or ocean
This was a great
discovery, in as-
much as the surplus pop-
ulation could be disposed
of in colonies as they became too numerous to dwell

IN AZATLAN

Hence was founded the Covenant of Azatlan, sometime called the everlasting covenant. (TRAGWITHL) The meaning of this word strictly is EXTREAN.

"AS LONG AS THE SIGNS APPEAR"...

The chief sign is the BULL. ('Bwla'—in the Kymrik) or TAURUS. The chief star in this sign is 'Aldebaran' (Bull's eye) = a rudy star. Opposite to this star in the heavens is the other rudy star 'Antares'. With the first is the full moon, and with the last, the sun. And MARS the rudy planet is the correspondent, or warior-king,

the movable star ~ allegorically, the agent that ex~
ecutes the decrees of the 3
kings, ORION

The three stars called the belt
of Orion are also called the 3
kings, representing three tribes
or nations in the Golden Land
or new Azatlan (Colonies)
that is, the continent that
then existed where now the
Pacific Ocean is.

In the islands of that ocean
at the present day, this
feast is yet observed.

At the Fiji Islands the ap~
pearance of these fish or worms

Travels to Sacred Sites
Wales/Teman

Excerpt from the Stone Books of Roberts:
"When they first arrived they found one
island in the center of the group, occupied
by a race of Giants, of which they had no
knowledge, this island was low and fertile
near the sea, with a high stone wall surround-
ing the whole, to keep out the sea from over-
flowing, the center was more elevated,
and near the center a circular hill, on top of
the hill a great boulder or rock, very smooth
and polished, it had many rooms or com-
partments, lighted by day and if dimly
through a frosted glass or horn but in the
night it was brilliant beyond description..
in the middle was the Great Oracle of Teman".
Bardsley Island

John Hugh Roberts
says:" Bardsley Island
is a famous place
in ancient history
a great resort
of the early saints
as well as
the Ancient Druids,
there is in it a
famous cave said
to reach the sea
to the sacred
Stonehouse (Teman)"

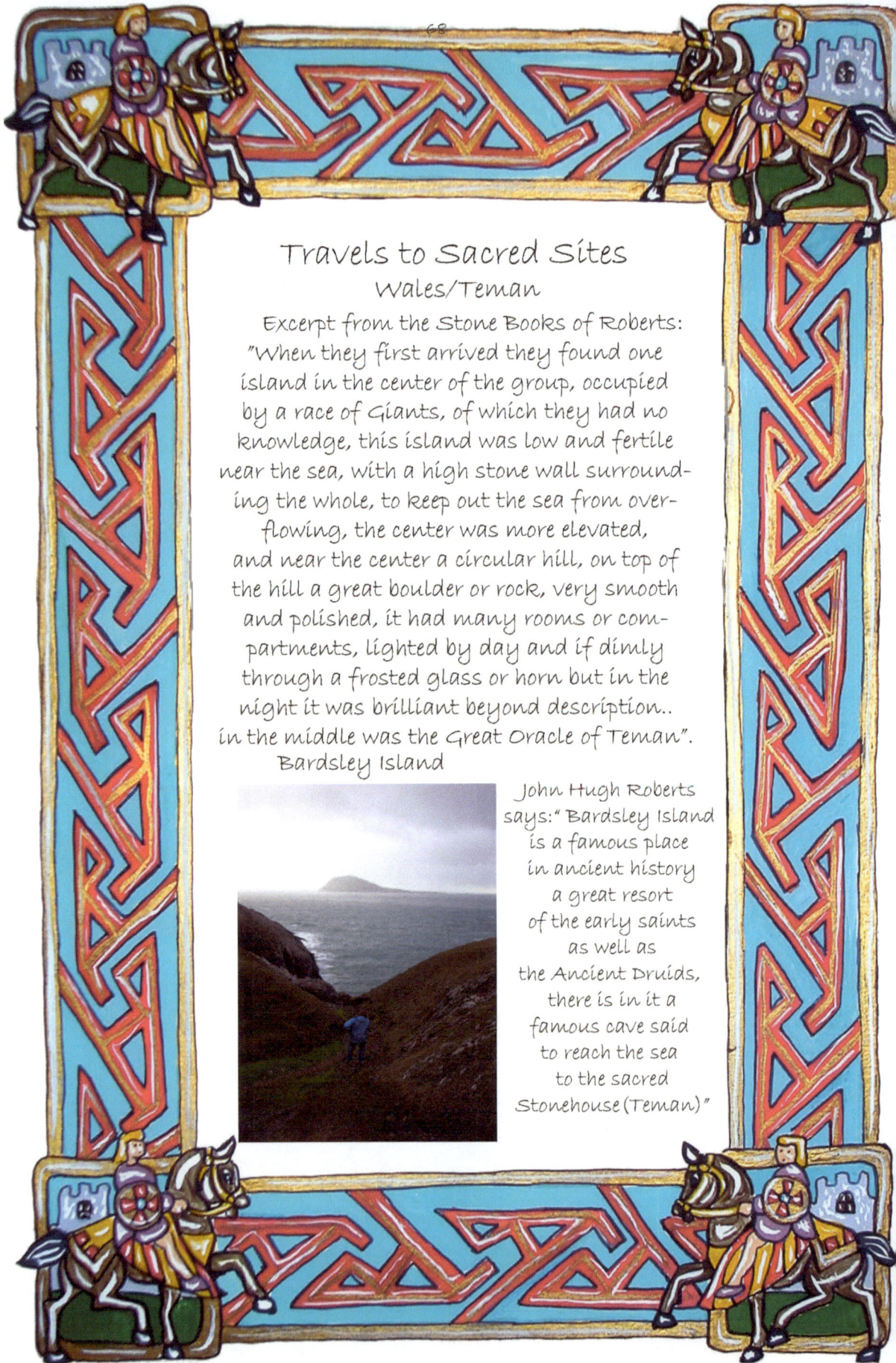

The mystical isle of Bardsley.

Illustration from the Stone Book of Knowledge
showing Teman

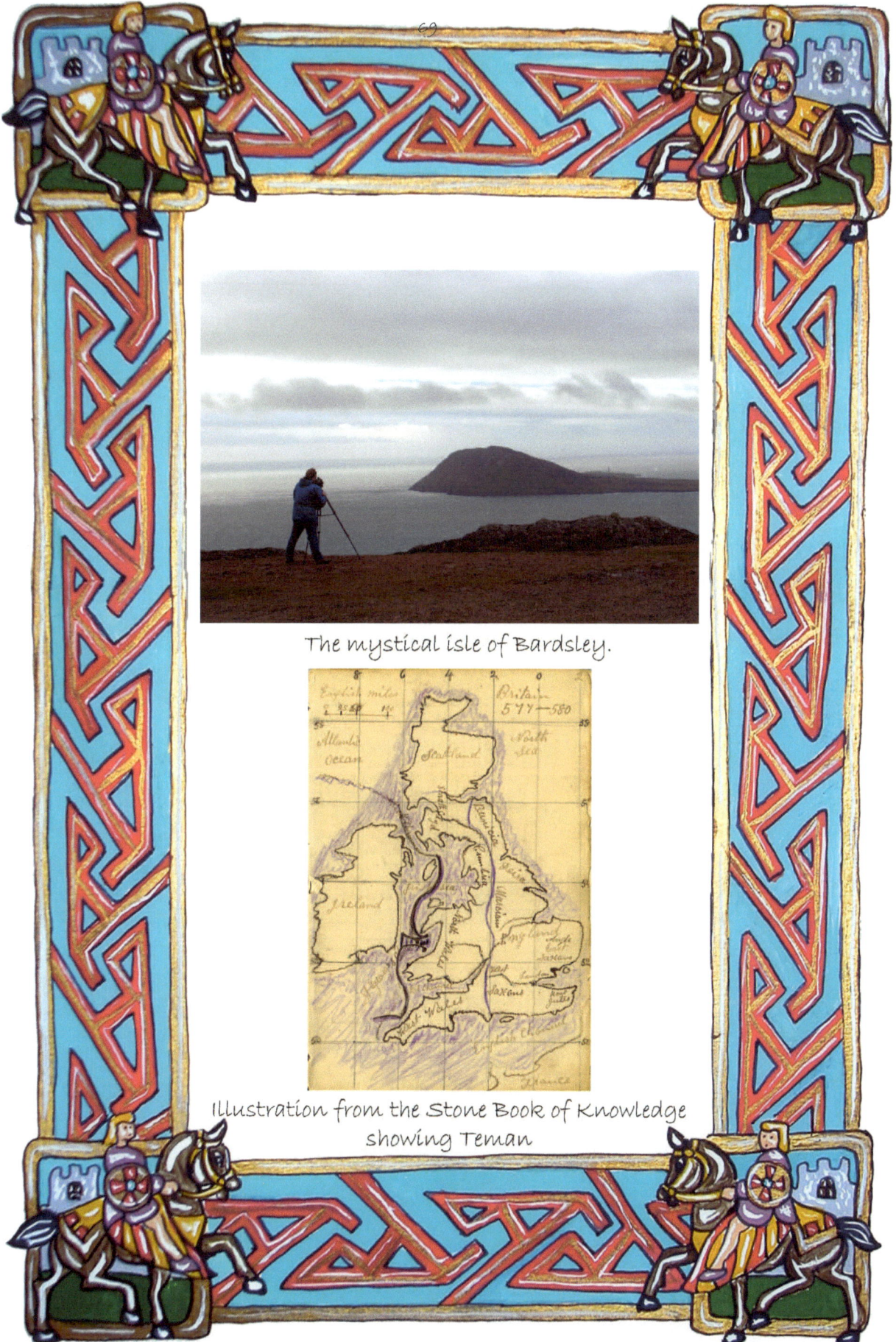

Peru

Excerpt from the paper on Madoc written
by John Hugh Roberts : "And now we must try the
fog and mist of time and more and endeavour
to rise above them, not on the mountains of
Europe but in America, in the year 1170 ano
Domini we are told the last Eisteddvod or
Congress of the Druids was held in Wales
according to the ancient prediction, the signs
of the times demanded the wihdrawal of certain
relics of the order from Wales where they were
guarded faithfully by the five Royal familys,
at the time (1186) Owain King of Gwynedd had them
in charge, two of his sons Howel and Madoc and
the ArchDruid were appointed to carry the relics
to Azatlan - this was sucessfully done."
It goes on to explain later his going back to Peru
and describes the building of the city of Cuzco where
the relics were deposited. "They must of known that the
longest elongation of the magnetic poles was over
Cuzco then or they would not have chosen the
place to deposit the relics"
I went to Peru to see what I could intuitively
find in Cuzco. At the archeological
Museum in Cuzco I found a broken bowl with runic
writings on it attributed to the twelfth century.
I also spoke to an educated Qchehcuan engineer who
showed me an entrance to an underground series of
caves that the native shamans used for certain ceremonies. These caves supposedly went on many
miles underground. This is still a mystery to
be unravelled.

Machu Picchu

One of the side trips from Cuzco was to Machu Picchu - one of the marvels of South America. Climbing Huachu Picchu, the high peak behind, was a feat that resulted in an incredible view of the ruins. It turns out that the top of Huachu was the site of the most important ceremonies. The carved stone steps leading up to the top were very, very narrow and not for the light-hearted.

Mexico

John Hugh Roberts in his writing mentions going to Mexico with two gentleman in 1846. He may have heard of Azatlan on this trip and continued to look for Azatlan through his life or maybe he knew of it before he went and so was searching. Whether he found it - this is a mystery. ???????????????

My wife and I were working in Mexico in 1998 and decided to visit the island of Mexicaltitlan also referred to as Azatlan. There was no cars on the island, the island is about 350 by 450 meters, so you could stand in the middle of the plaza and look straight across the island in each direction. The streets went around the center in circles forming a great mandala. We visited the Museo "El Orgin" and saw photographs of the old maps of the island and a stone sculpture which told the story of how the Mexican people were shown in a vision of Huitzilopochtli to find an eagle holding a snake in its beak. We were told they apparently left the island and walked a long time and finally saw an eagle with a snake in its beak over a lake. Here they built Tenochtitlan, home of the Aztecs that later became Mexico City.

A few years later I visited CHICHEN ITZA another sacred site for inspiration-here something special happens on the spring equinox!

Inside the inner pyramid at CHICHEN ITZA

The pyramid CHICHEN ITZA,
Yucatan Mexico

England- Stonehenge & Avebury

Excerpt from the old manuscripts of Roberts:
There are listed:
"The three mighty works of Britian
— to set up the Ketti Stones, to build
Stonehenge, and to bring together
Kludair Guvrangaon".
with the Roberts writing we have 55 years
of his dairies and in one entry he speaks of
going to visit Stonehenge in the 1840's.
The power of this sacred site remains today.
When living in England we visited
Stonehenge - it was amazing in that
it showed the important alignments of the
sun and moon. Near Stonehenge is another
sacred site, Avebury where each of the huge
monoliths seem to take on a spiritual power
of its own, each one as if alive. The configurat-
ion of the sun and moon stone circles is quite
over-powering.

Stonehenge at sunrise

Some of the wonderful stones at Avebury

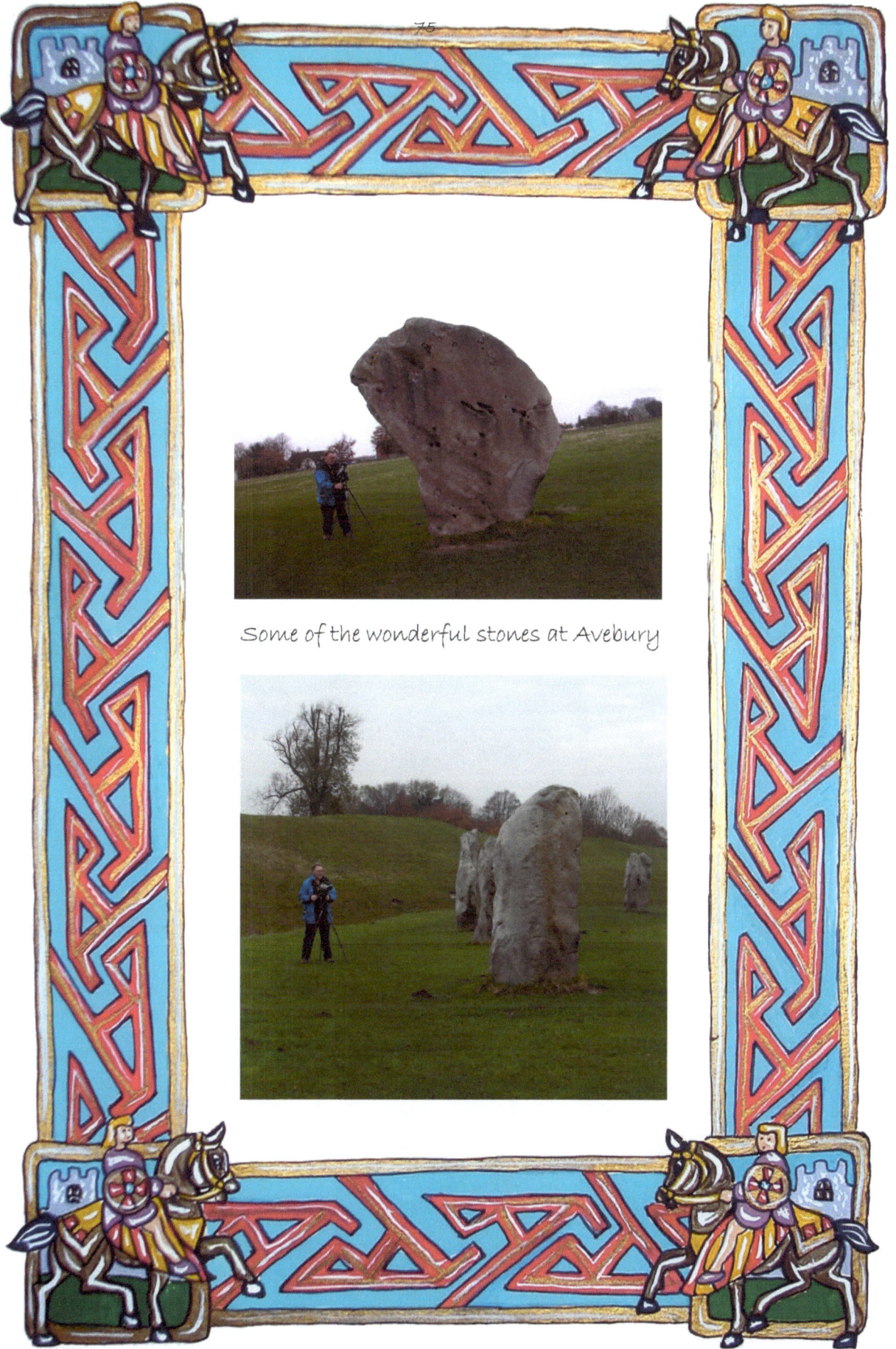

England - Cornwall

The power of the sacred sites continues to draw me to them. In Cornwall the syncronicity continued as our guide Barbara Tremain, a psychic, directed us to certain sacred places after reading the manuscripts. One such place was Bocsacwen-Un where all the evidence indicated was the stone circle Roberts performed Druid rituals at in the 1830's. She also took us to a place nearby on the seashore where she felt the Three Mermaids ceremonies would of taken place.

Bocsacwen-Un , Cornwall

Were mermaids here?

Ireland - New Grange

Another sacred place of inspiration was New Grange in Ireland. This was particularly special to me because of my Irish heritage. It is a remarkable engineering feat proven to be over 5750 years old. There is an opening over the doorway at the front facing south east, where, on the winter solstice, at dawn the light comes through the opening and lights up the floor of the inner chamber over 100 feet into the mound. Around the perimeter of this mound are large inscribed monoliths lying on their sides with remarkable designs of whorls and zoomorphic images. White quartz outlines the entranceway, Stunningly beautiful!

New Grange, Ireland

After these many years I have realized that these records are for those searching for truth – Through visiting many of the sacred sites in Cornwall, Wales, Scotland, and Ireland, along with sites in Peru and Mexico, I have discovered connections Roberts alluded to in his writings. The further I studied these remarkable papers the more I learned to trust my intuition - I know messages in these writings will strengthen many people searching for their own truths.

Here I am planning future Druidical Quest Projects

We are presently planning a drama/documentary of the Druidical Quest along with plans to publish the full 254 pages of the Stone Book of Knowledge with a further 100 pages of further Drudical writings of Roberts. We hope also to publish the full size Illuminations of Leo Del Pasqua's 1982 work of the four papers shown here in this book. The size of the originals are 9' 3/8" in x 12 1/2" in. With over 15 hours of video of many of the places that Roberts mentions in the papers we want to develop an interactive DVD for people to further discover elements of his wonderful records of 7400 years.

Carn Fadryn, Lleyn, Gwynedd, a very special place.

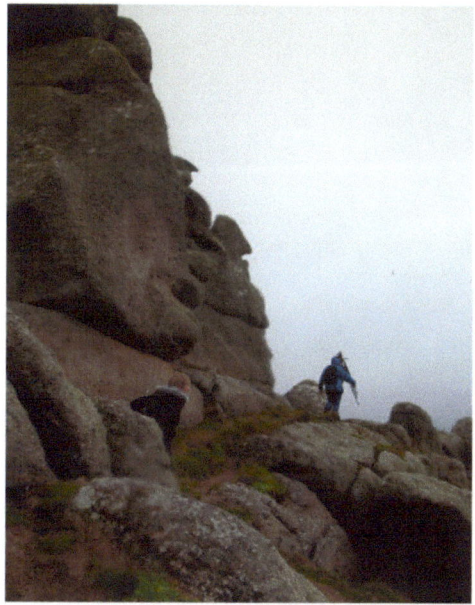

The Rock formations at Lands End, Cornwall

The last Time I saw David Davies was when he stuck his arm out of his Morris Minor and with his arm extending striaght up out of the window said, 'Dale, there's one last word, "Excalibre", and off he drove while I turned and walked to the foot of Skiridd Fawr climbing the Holy mountain to initiate a sacred pipe given to me by my mentor Dr. H. Binder.

At the close of the pipe ceremony I saw a vision of a whale tail fin that changed into a crest of water – huge like a 300 foot tidal wave. A sense of well being permeated through my being with the sight of this vision and then a large old wise bald headed eagle landed in front of me at a distance and proceeded to look me straight in the eye, prancing with wings outstretched and it danced before me. I then flashed on a white eagle dance done by the White Eagle Azteca Dance Group that I had seen in 1982 A second vision came to me days later. It was as follows: White Buffalo vision – full moon night – a guide showed us a spot for a quest – late morning vision came as a white buffalo surrounded by a rainbow and at that moment I realized I was to work and guide young people in the ancient ways of self healing and self discovery using the knowledge of the Native Shamanism, Druidism and Buddhism.

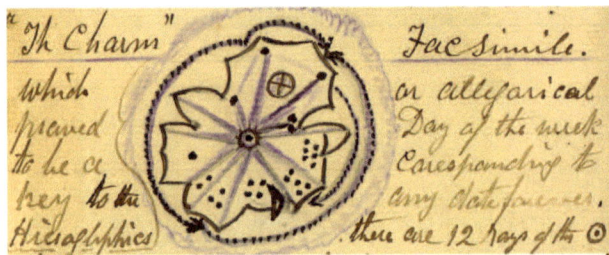

"Th Charm" Fac simile. which proaned to be ce key to the Hieroglyphics

on allegorical Day of the week Caresponding to any date forever. there are 12 days of the ☉

The Key!
May Your Journey also be full of wonder!
Dale Bertrand

Leo Del Pasqua

Leo did all the wonderful illuminations of the Druid
manuscripts. He is a Practicing Symbolist
with a specific interest in contemporary
Spiritual Art. He holds a Master's Degree
in Theology from the University of Toronto.

Examples of his artwork and poetry may be viewed
at Urantia's "Brother Leo's corner"
on line. Leo also has Ebays
Veronicas Liturgical Art and hosts the
Radio program "Church of the Earth"
on CHCR 102.0 FM Community Radio in Killaloe
on Sunday
afternoon.

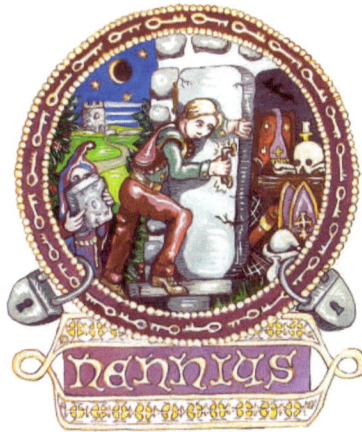

nannius

Dale Bertrand

Dale is a lover of the mystical and magical in life. He has travelled extensively fulfilling his quest for knowledge. He has worked in public & private enterprises as a policeman, photographer, various management positions in retail, wholesale, manufacturing and service industry, workshop leadership, and the last ten years teaching and developing courses in E.S.L., Speech Presentation and Business Economics. He loves ethnographic antiques and was part of the management team at the Toronto Harbourfront Antique Market for seven years during the eighties. He helped co-author 'The Environmental Activity Guide' which has been workshoped in many schools and has designed websites – including two of his own– www.dodoland.com and www.azatlan.com. Researching the Druid manuscripts and diaries has taken him a dozen times to Wales, and also Ireland, Scotland, Cornwall and in following up on some of the more unusual leads he has travelled to Peru, Guatemala, and Mexico. Currently he is developing a film outline for the project to also include theatrical and interactive DVD applications and is open to collaboration for further development of the project.